My Millionaire Routine

ISBN 979-8-88796-879-7 (Paperback)
ISBN: 070-8-88796-870-4 (Ebook)

Disclaimer: This is a work of fiction. Any resemblance to actual events or persons, living or dead, is entirely coincidental.

Editing by Book Baby
Illustrated by Nad-Arts
Self- Publish by Shareka Thomas

Limitations live only in our minds.
But if we use our imaginations, our
possibilities become limitless.

– JAMIE PAOLINETTI

I know I can be where I want to be! If I work hard at it, I'll be where I want to be.

So, I get plenty of rest; sleep increases my learning ability, my attention span, and my overall growth.

I know I can be where I want to be! If I work hard at it, I'll be where I want to be.

So, I get plenty of rest; sleep increases my learning ability, my attention span, and my overall growth .

I know I can be where I want to be! If I work hard at it, I'll be where I want to be.

So, I meditate before starting my day; meditation improves my
concentration and focus.

I know I can be where I want to be! If I work hard at it, I'll be where I want to be.

So, I exercise every day; whether I walk, run,
do jumping jacks, or pushups, confidence
and self-love help you face your fears.

I know I can be where I want to be! If I work hard at
it, I'll be where I want to be.

So, I always make sure I eat my fruits and vegetables;
your health is your wealth.

I know I can be where I want to be! If I work hard at it, I'll be where I want to be.

So, I read as much as possible, whether it's one page or one book, leaders read.

I know I can be where I want to be! If I work hard at it, I'll be where I want to be.

So, I set daily goals for myself to complete;
a goal without a timeline is just a dream.

Goals

I know I can be where I want to be! If I work hard at it, I'll be where I want to be.

So, I take school seriously; knowledge is power, and what you don't know can sometimes hurt you.

I know I can be where I want to be! If I work hard at it, I'll be where I want to be.

So, I have mentors; mentors are beneficial for providing information and knowledge about a particular subject, so surround yourself with people on the same mission as you.

I know I can be where I want to be! If I work hard at
it, I'll be where I want to be.

So, I save 20 percent of anything I earn; always pay you first, do not save what is left after spending; spend what is left after saving.

I know I can be where I want to be! If I work hard at it, I'll be where I want to be.

So, I created a vision board; a comfort zone is a beautiful place, but nothing ever grows there. Know your limits then ignore them and hold that vision!

Vision Board

I know I can be where I want to be! If I work hard at it, I'll be where I want to be.

So, I network with others; sometimes it's not what you know but who you know.

I know I can be where I want to be! If I work hard at it, I'll be where I want to be.

So, I block out negative self-talk; you must be careful how you talk to yourself, because you are always listening.
"I'm not listening"

I know I can be where I want to be! If I work hard at
it, I'll be where I want to be.

Fail at something new as much as possible; failure is a part of success, and we learn from failure, not success.

I know I can be where I want to be! If I work hard at it, I'll be where I want to be.

"I can do anything"
You are right, say it louder!

I know I can be where I want to be! If I work hard at it, I'll be where I want to be.

"louder"
I really wasn´t convinced;
say it louder this time!

I know I can be where I want to be! If I work hard at it, I'll be where I want to be.

Stop what you're doing! Go look in the mirror and say it as loud as you can.

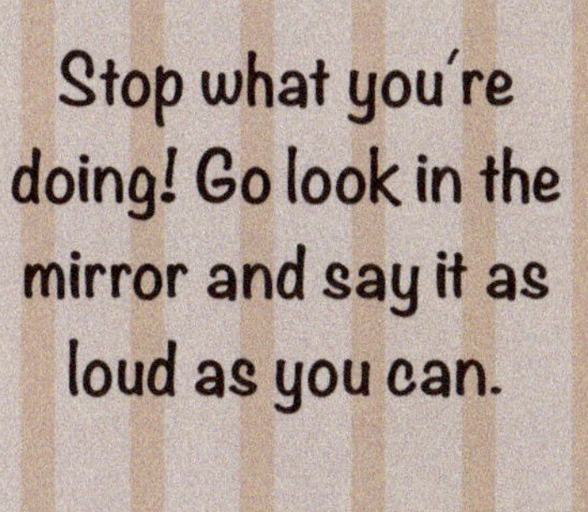

I know I can be where I want to be! If I work hard at it, I'll be where I want to be.

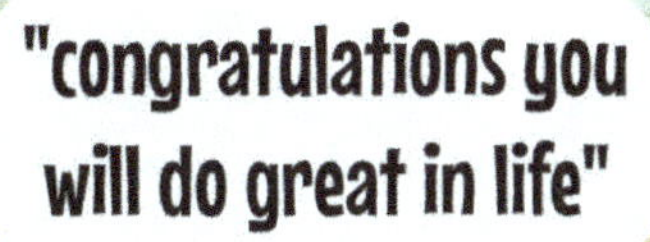

Okay, okay I believe you now, and it sounds like you believe in you, too. Just remember, you can do anything, and you can be anything, as long as you believe in yourself and work hard until you get there.

Mindset Fresh Book Collection

This wonderful book collection is available in two formats. Ebook (Amazon Kindle) & paperback in over 450 book retailers, bookstores, and libraries all over the US and other territories, so make sure you visit your nearby bookstore in person or shop online at our website https://mindsetfreshstroes.com/ and cop yours today

Litty & The Giant

Print ISBN 978-1-63848-383-0
Ebook ISBN 978-1-63848-384-7

Blue & Wormy Self-Love Stroll to School

Print ISBN 978-1-0879-8363-9
Ebook ISBN 978-1-0879-8360-8

On My Journey 2 Greatness

Print ISBN 978-1-63848-386-1
Ebook ISBN 978-1-63901-912-0

Mindset Fresh 31 Day Reflection Journal

Print ISBN 978-1-63877-967-1
Ebook ISBN 978-1-63877-969-8

Mindset Fresh Kid's Reflection Journal

Print ISBN 978-1-63877-955-1
Ebook ISBN 978-1-63877-956-8

My Favorite Apple Tree

Print ISBN 979-8-88589-637-5
Ebook ISBN 979-8-88589-638-2

Biography

Shareka Thomas challenges people of all ages to live out their own "Phenomenal Self". Her motivation comes from childhood experiences, as there were times where she struggled with self- doubt, fear and adversity. Over the years she has overcame those barriers through prayer, listing to motivational speakers, changing her perspective, facing her fears and speaking nothing but positivity into her life existence.

She loves to share her story and encourage others to discover their superpower and climb endless stairs of possibilities. She believes that if you walk by faith and not by sight nothing is impossible. If you can dream it, you can achieve it